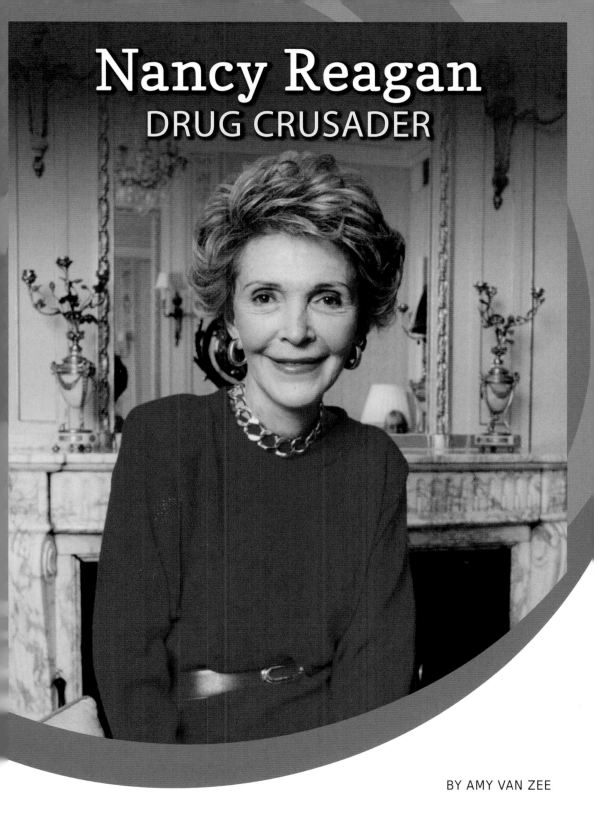

Nancy Reagan
DRUG CRUSADER

BY AMY VAN ZEE

Published by The Child's World®
1980 Lookout Drive • Mankato, MN 56003-1705
800-599-READ • www.childsworld.com

ISBN 9781503824034
LCCN 2017944743

Printed in the United States of America
PA02362

ABOUT THE AUTHOR

Amy Van Zee is an editor and writer who lives with her family near Minneapolis, Minnesota. She has an English degree from the University of Minnesota and has contributed to dozens of educational books.

TABLE OF
CONTENTS

FAST FACTS

Full Name

- Anne Frances "Nancy" Robbins Davis Reagan

Birthdate

- July 6, 1921, in New York City, New York

Husband

- President Ronald Wilson Reagan

Children

- Patti Davis and Ron Reagan

Years in White House

- 1981–1989

Accomplishments

- Raised money to **renovate** the White House in 1981.
- Promoted the **Foster** Grandparent Program, which paired volunteers older than 55 with special-needs youth.
- Traveled, wrote, and spoke out against drug and alcohol abuse, especially among young people.

Chapter 1

PROTECTOR OF THE PRESIDENT

ancy Reagan ran down the hall to the hospital room. Inside was her husband, President Ronald Reagan. He was in terrible condition. Glancing in the corner, Nancy saw that Ronald's brand-new blue suit lay bloodied and torn. Nurses and doctors were rushing to **stabilize** her husband. It was March 30, 1981, and Ronald had been shot.

The president was taken to an operating room. During the surgery, Nancy prayed Ronald would **survive**. The surgeons were able to remove the bullet. They found it one inch from the president's heart.

◄ Nancy supported Ronald through several health struggles during his presidency.

Over the following months, Ronald slowly built up his strength. But Nancy did not soon forget what had happened to her beloved husband. She later wrote, "I now understood that each new day was a gift to be treasured, and that I had to be more involved in seeing that my husband was protected in every possible way."[1]

So Nancy made it her job to be her husband's biggest protector. From then on, she wanted to know where Ronald was, with whom he was meeting, and at what time. Nancy and Ronald spent most of their free time together. The president greatly relied on his First Lady.

Nancy and Ronald had met in California in 1951. Nancy was working as an actress. Ronald was an actor and president of the Screen Actors **Guild**.

"I've said it before and I'll say it once again: My life didn't really begin until I met Ronnie."[2]

—*Nancy Reagan*

▲ Nancy and Ronald celebrated his nomination for governor of California in 1966.

They married on March 4, 1952. Nancy was completely devoted to her husband. She later wrote, "Yes, almost from the day I met him, Ronald Reagan has been the center of my life."[3]

Ronald gave up acting and went into politics. In 1966, Ronald was elected governor of California. With Nancy by his side, he served for eight years. Nancy was a strong supporter of Ronald and made appearances for him during the **campaign**. Nancy found campaigning to be interesting. And there would be more of it ahead as her husband sought the presidency.

Chapter 2

A NEW HOME, A NEW LIFE

Tears filled Nancy's eyes. In a few moments, her life would change forever. She stood next to Ronald, facing west. Her red coat and hat stood out boldly in the mild, gray winter day. It was **inauguration** day, January 20, 1981. Nancy was about to become First Lady of the United States.

After Ronald's speech, a special lunch, and a parade, the Reagans went to ten different balls. Then they returned to the White House, which was now their home. Nancy later wrote, "You think about all the families who have lived here before. It's very humbling."[4]

◄ Nancy and Ronald waved to a crowd of people after Ronald became the 40th president.

But when Nancy first toured the White House before moving in, she felt that it was "dreary and uninviting."[5] To her, the rooms were not suited for hosting presidential events. She wrote, "I have always felt that the White House should be magnificent, and I made up my mind that as soon as we moved in I would fix it up."[6]

Nancy raised money to renovate the White House. Walls were repainted, and wallpaper was installed. Floors and doors were sanded and refinished, and new carpet was put down. Antique furnishings were brought in. With the White House transformed, Nancy put it to good use. She understood that hosting **formal** events would be a big part of her role as First Lady.

"While the president's job is clearly defined, nobody really knows exactly what the First Lady is supposed to do. . . . Each incoming First Lady has had to define the job for herself."[7]

—Nancy Reagan

▲ Nancy hosted events for world leaders, such as Queen Elizabeth II (second from right) and Prince Philip (left), during her time as First Lady.

She chose to be very involved in the details of each event, big or small. In their eight years in the White House, Nancy hosted many parties. Her style was more formal than that of former First Ladies.

But Nancy did not spend all her time in the White House. She also worked with the Foster Grandparent Program (FGP). This program pairs volunteers age 55 and older with special-needs youth. Through the FGP, Nancy saw the benefits of having a loving, devoted older adult in the life of a child. She wrote, "It seems a fact of nature that the very young and the very old cannot resist the warmth offered each to the other."[8] Nancy became a great **advocate** for the program. She co-wrote a book sharing stories of FGP participants. With her support, the FGP grew.

◄ Nancy promoted her book, *To Love a Child*, which was published in 1982.

Chapter 3

A DRUG-FREE AMERICA

Nancy and Ronald sat next to each other on the small sofa, holding hands. They were in the West Hall of the White House. It was September 14, 1986, and the president and First Lady were talking to the nation on television.

When it was Nancy's turn, she looked directly into the camera. She spoke openly about drug abuse in the United States. She was especially concerned about how drugs affected youth. Nancy spoke about her travels around the United States, talking with people about drugs.

◄ Nancy gave speeches across the country to promote her "Just Say No" campaign, which tried to fight drug abuse.

During the television address, Nancy spoke directly to young people. She said, "Say yes to your life. And when it comes to drugs and alcohol, just say no."[9]

Throughout her years in the White House, Nancy used her influence to take a stand against drugs. The "Just Say No" campaign became one of Nancy's biggest causes. She visited schools, wrote articles, gave speeches, and went on television to promote drug education. In 1985, she hosted an international drug abuse awareness conference at the White House. First Ladies from 17 countries attended. By 1988, more than 12,000 "Just Say No" clubs had been formed around the world.

> "Drugs take away the dream from every child's heart and replace it with a nightmare, and it's time we in America stand up and replace those dreams."[10]
>
> —Nancy Reagan

Nancy discussed the country's drug problem at ▶ a White House meeting in 1982.

▲ Nancy laid her hand on Ronald's casket
at his funeral in 2004.

The Reagans left the White House in 1989 and
returned to California. Years later, in 1994, Ronald was
diagnosed with **Alzheimer's disease**.

Nancy continued to care for Ronald with great attention and love. He died in 2004. Nancy died on March 6, 2016, in California. Just as she had planned her events in the White House, Nancy planned the details of her own funeral. She was buried next to her beloved Ronald, facing west to look out over the Pacific Ocean.

THINK ABOUT IT

- Nancy wrote that each First Lady has to define the role for herself. What do you think are important parts of a First Lady's role?
- Nancy raised funds from donors to renovate the White House. Who do you think should pay for the White House's renovations? The family living in it, donors, or US taxpayers? Why?
- How do you think Ronald's shooting affected Nancy's feelings about her husband's job as president?
- How did Nancy's work in the White House impact the nation?

GLOSSARY

advocate (AD-vuh-kit): An advocate is a person who stands for something. Nancy was an advocate for the Foster Grandparent Program.

Alzheimer's disease (AWLTS-hye-murz duh-ZEEZ): Alzheimer's disease affects a person's brain, resulting in memory loss. Ronald was diagnosed with Alzheimer's disease in 1994.

campaign (kam-PAYN): A campaign is when a person works toward being elected. Nancy helped Ronald during his campaign.

formal (FOR-mul): Formal means fancy or elaborate. Nancy hosted many formal events at the White House.

foster (FOSS-tur): To foster is to care for another person who is not related by blood. The Foster Grandparent Program matched young people with older volunteers.

guild (GILD): A guild is a group of people with similar interests or jobs. Ronald was the president of the Screen Actors Guild.

inauguration (in-aw-gyuh-RAY-shun): An inauguration is a special ceremony in which a new president takes office. Nancy wore a bright-red coat and hat to her husband's inauguration.

renovate (REN-uh-vate): To renovate is to fix up a house or property. Nancy worked hard and raised money to renovate the White House.

stabilize (STAY-bul-ize): To stabilize is to make something steady. When Ronald was shot, doctors and nurses worked to stabilize him.

survive (sur-VIVE): To survive is to live. Nancy prayed her husband would survive after he was shot.

SOURCE NOTES

1. Nancy Reagan. *My Turn: The Memoirs of Nancy Reagan*. New York, NY: Random House, 1989. Print. 17.

2. Ibid. 93.

3. Ibid. viii.

4. Ibid. 236.

5. Ibid. 225.

6. Ibid.

7. Ibid. 57.

8. Nancy Reagan. *To Love a Child*. Indianapolis, IN: Bobbs-Merrill, 1982. Print. xiii.

9. "President Reagan's Address to the Nation on the Campaign against Drug Abuse—9/14/86." *Reagan Foundation*. YouTube, 3 Aug. 2011. Web. 10 July 2017.

10. Ibid.

TO LEARN MORE

Books

Duffield, Katy S. *Ronald Reagan*. Mankato, MN: The Child's World, 2017.

Gigliotti, Jim. *Ronald Reagan, the 40th President*. New York, NY: Bearport Publishing, 2017.

Pastan, Amy. *First Ladies*. New York, NY: DK Publishing, 2017.

Web Sites

Visit our Web site for links about Nancy Reagan:
childsworld.com/links

Note to Parents, Teachers, and Librarians: We routinely verify our Web links to make sure they are safe and active sites. So encourage your readers to check them out!

INDEX